Kingdom Kids Create™

KENYA

Fruit of the Spirit

Kingdom Kids Create

First Edition.
ISBN: 978-1-947303-08-9
Printed in the USA.

How to Use This Book

Step #1:   Read the devotion with your child, grandchild, or group of children.

Step #2:   Use a QR code reader app (easily downloaded from your app store or Google Play store on your smart phone) and the QR code (it looks like this: ▦) located at the end of each devotion to play the video from the kids from Kenya.

Step #3: Take time to discuss the questions at the end of the devotion. Talking about God's word is a wonderful way to spend time together

Step #4: Either purchase beaded bracelets at www.kingdomkidscreate.com (made by the kids in Kenya) or make your own beaded bracelets together with your children to act as a reminder of each of the Fruit of the Spirit.

Have fun and make wonderful memories!

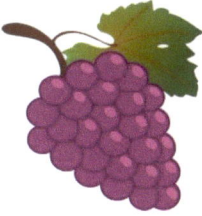

Fruit of the Spirit:
LOVE

Hello there, boys and girls!
My name is Susan Wambui.

I live in Nyahururu, Kenya in Africa at The Home of the Good Shepherd. Today I would like to share with you what I have learned about LOVE by living with many other children.

PRAYER

Let's open with a short prayer:

Lord God, please give us ears to hear you speaking to us through this devotional and a heart that is willing to learn. Amen.

DEVOTIONAL

You see I have lots of brothers and sisters and every day I choose to behave in a loving way towards them. There are times when I would rather do something for myself, or just do nothing at all, but I do not choose to. Instead, I choose LOVE. There are times when I make a bad choice, but when I do, I ask for forgiveness and ask for help in making a better choice next time. Without the help of God, the Father, Son, and Holy Spirit, I could not succeed.

Let's look at God's word and see what it says about LOVE. Let's try to memorize this verse in 1 Corinthians 13.

MEMORY VERSE

"Love cares more for others than it does for self." (1 Corinthians 13:5 MSG)

POEM

Another fun way to learn about LOVE is to read through this poem. Poems help us remember.

Jesus tells us to LOVE ourselves
and to LOVE each other.
To treat everyone like a friend
as a sister or a brother.

To LOVE everyone that cares for us
is an easy thing to do.
But Jesus wants us to LOVE even those
that are not nice to you.

That can be really hard
and may not sound very fair.
Why should we have to LOVE someone
that doesn't even care?

The answer to that question is easy
and something we all need to know.
We must LOVE each other
because Jesus said so.

To help us when loving others
is not something we want to do,
Jesus sent His Holy Spirit
to be a guide for me and you.

When loving someone is difficult
and you would rather just walk away,
Think about Jesus and remember
the words He had to say.

LOVE is Patient; LOVE is Kind.
So, follow Jesus and always keep
LOVE on your heart and mind.

Very good boys and girls! Thank you for
joining us today all the way in Kenya!

PRAYER

Before we go, can we pray together and ask
for God's help in choosing to live a life of
LOVE?

Lord God,

Thank you that you are LOVE. Thank you for sending me the example of unselfish LOVE by sending Jesus. Thank you for giving me your Spirit to help me be loving. I need your help every day to LOVE others more than I LOVE myself. Helping others is a nice thought, but I need your help to actually do it. Show me how you want me to help others this week. Holy Spirit give me the power to act on what the Lord shows me. In Jesus' name, I pray all these things. Amen.

Discussion questions for parents and grandparents with their children and grandchildren:

🍇 What is the first thing that comes to mind when you ask God to show you something loving to do for someone else?

🍇 Will you commit to doing it?

Here's a fun idea: You can use a purple beaded bracelet to remind you of God's LOVE for you and to share His LOVE with others. If you don't have one, you can make your own bracelet with purple beads.

Enjoy watching a video of this devotion online by using this link:
https://vimeo.com/198359203

Or by scanning the QR code below

Fruit of the Spirit:
JOY

Hello there, boys and girls!
My name is Lilian Wambui.

I live in Nyahururu, Kenya in Africa at The Home of the Good Shepherd. Today I would like to share with you what I have learned about JOY by living with many other children.

PRAYER

Let's open with a short prayer:

Lord God, please give us ears to hear you speaking to us through this devotional and a heart that is willing to learn. Amen.

DEVOTIONAL

You already know I have lots of brothers and sisters. That means many times a day there is a way for me to share my JOY with someone. Do you know what it means to share JOY? It is way more than just being happy, because I can have JOY even if my day is not going well. You can too! Even though we can't see Him, JOY comes from believing in Jesus.

When we believe in Jesus, God fills us with His gift of JOY. Jesus saved us from our troubles, so that is great reason to be joyful! I also don't keep JOY to myself. I love to share it with others by singing, dancing and smiling at everyone. Just like with showing LOVE, I

need the help of God, the Father, Son, and Holy Spirit or I could not succeed.
Let's look at God's word and see what it says about JOY. Let's try to memorize this verse in 1 Peter 1.

MEMORY VERSE

"Though you have not seen him, you love him; and even though you do not see him now, you believe in him and are filled with an inexpressible and glorious joy."
(1 Peter 1:8)

POEM

Another fun way to learn about JOY is to read through this poem. Poems help us remember.

A piece of candy can make you happy
but it does not last very long.
Having JOY in your heart is like singing
a never-ending song.
Happiness is temporary

but JOY is with you each and every day.
When the sun is shining, or rain is falling
JOY gives you the words to pray.

Thanking Jesus for all the blessings
He has freely given you,
For the gift of JOY and love of the Holy Spirit
that will see you through.

So, when you are happy or when you are sad
lift your voice in highest praise.
Give thanks to Jesus for the JOY that is with
you throughout all your days.

PRAYER

Before we go, can we pray together and ask
for God's help in choosing to share our JOY?

Lord God,

Thank you that you freely give us JOY as we
believe in Your Son, Jesus. Thank you for
giving me your Spirit to help me have JOY. I
need your help every day to share JOY with

others. Help me to continue to sing, dance and smile so that your JOY in me is plain to see by everyone I am around. Show me new ways to share your JOY in me with others this week. Holy Spirit give me the power to act on what the Lord shows me. In Jesus name, I pray all these things. Amen.

Discussion questions for parents and grandparents with their children and grandchildren:

What is the first thing that comes to mind when you ask God to show you a way to share JOY with others?

Will you commit to doing it?

Here's a fun idea: You can use a bright red beaded bracelet to remind you of God's JOY for you and to share His JOY with others. If you don't have one, you can make your own bracelet with red beads.

Enjoy watching a video of this devotion online
by using this link:
https://vimeo.com/201669759
Or by scanning the QR code below:

Fruit of the Spirit:
PEACE

Hello there, boys and girls!
My name is Hamisa Wambui.

I live in Nyahururu, Kenya in Africa at The Home of the Good Shepherd. Today I would like to share with you what I have learned about PEACE by living with many other children.

PRAYER

Let's open with a short prayer:

Lord God, please give us ears to hear you speaking to us through this devotional and a heart that is willing to learn. Amen.

DEVOTIONAL

My life at The Home of the Good Shepherd is full of PEACE. You see, God's PEACE is different than the PEACE the world talks about. The world's PEACE is based on everything going well around us, but God's PEACE is always with us, no matter what is happening in the world, in Kenya, in school or at home. Do you want to know why? It is because PEACE is a gift to us from God, given to us through Christ, and is available to us daily through the Holy Spirit's work inside of us. So that means we don't have to work at having PEACE; we just have to receive it as a gift from God. Isn't that wonderful? So, if I get afraid of the dark at night, get worried about my grades in school or get angry with a brother or sister, I can ask the Holy Spirit to fill me with God's PEACE. Then the fear and worry will disappear as quickly as I can blink my eye and others will feel peaceful when they are around me. Just like with JOY, I always need the help of God the Father, Son and Holy Spirit or I could not succeed.

Let's look at God's word and see what it says about PEACE. Let's try to memorize this verse in John 14.

MEMORY VERSE

"Peace I leave with you; my peace I give you. I do not give to you as the world gives. Do not let your hearts be troubled and do not be afraid." (John 14:27)

POEM

Another fun way to learn about PEACE is to read through this poem. Poems help us remember.

PEACE in your heart, PEACE in your home
PEACE in everywhere you go.
This is what Jesus wants you to have
and wants you to show.

When you have LOVE and JOY in your heart
PEACE will be there too.
Then you can share this PEACE with others
as Jesus has with you.

PEACE is much like LOVE and JOY
as it is good in every way.
Sharing PEACE with others is the best way
to live your life each and every day.

When you are not feeling PEACE in your life
take a moment to pray,
Letting Jesus and the Holy Spirit give you
PEACE
as you go on your way.

PRAYER

Before we go, can we pray together and ask
for God's help in choosing to share our
PEACE?

Lord God,

Thank you that you freely give us PEACE as we believe in your Son, Jesus. Thank you for giving me your Spirit to help me have PEACE. I need your help every day to live in PEACE with others. Help me to remember to ask you for your PEACE anytime I am afraid, worried or angry. Show me new ways to live in PEACE with others. Holy Spirit give me the power to act on what the Lord shows me. In Jesus' name, I pray all these things. Amen.

Discussion questions for parents and grandparents with their children and grandchildren:

🔮 What is the first thing that comes to mind when you ask God to show you a way to live in PEACE with yourself and with others?

🔮 Will you commit to doing it?

Here's a fun idea: You can use a light purple beaded bracelet to remind you of God's PEACE for you and to share His PEACE with others. If you don't have one, you can make your own bracelet with light purple beads.

Enjoy watching a video of this devotion online by using this link:
https://vimeo.com/201669759

Or by scanning the QR code below

Fruit of the Spirit:
PATIENCE

Hello there, boys and girls!
My name is Joyce Wairimu.

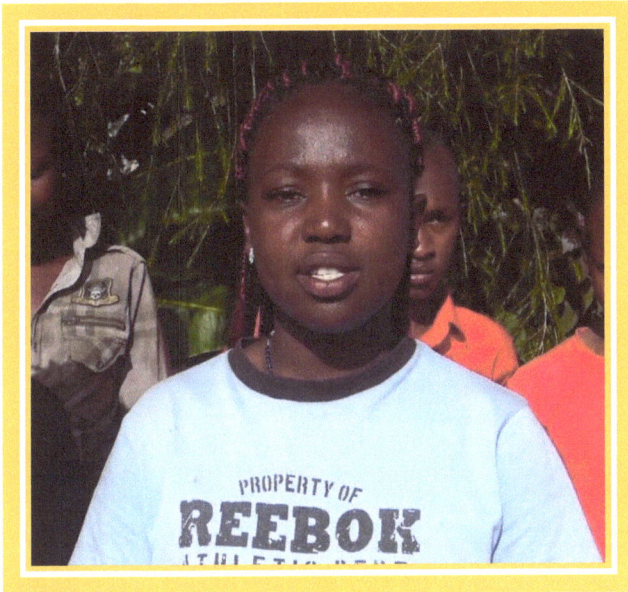

I live in Nyahururu, Kenya in Africa at The
Home of the Good Shepherd. Today I would
like to share with you what I have learned
about PATIENCE by living with many other
children.

PRAYER

Let's open with a short prayer:

Lord God, please give us ears to hear you speaking to us through this devotional and a heart that is willing to learn. Amen.

DEVOTIONAL

Since I live with so many brothers and sisters, there are many times that I must have PATIENCE. Do you know what it means to have PATIENCE? PATIENCE is going through something very hard, or just something very annoying, without getting angry or complaining. I must have PATIENCE oftentimes at dinner because there are so many of us eating and I am so hungry after a long day at school. I also must have PATIENCE when doing my homework or chores because I would rather be playing outside.

During these times, it helps me to remember how much PATIENCE God has with me. He could be angry with me so many times, but He isn't. He always loves me no matter what. He loves you no matter what you do too. He sent His Son, Jesus, to save you and me from our sins and He gave us the Holy Spirit to live in us to be our guide and helper. Thanks be to God because without Him I could not succeed.

Let's look at God's word and see what it says about PATIENCE. Let's try to memorize this verse in Colossians 1.

MEMORY VERSE

"Being strengthened with all power according to HIS glorious might so that you may have great endurance and patience."
(Colossians 1:11)

POEM

Another fun way to learn about PATIENCE is to read through this poem. Poems help us remember.

Jesus says PATIENCE is one way
to show our love to others.
Showing PATIENCE to our friends, family,
sisters and brothers.

When others are not being kind
or treating you with respect and love,
Call upon Jesus and the Holy Spirit
to give you the PATIENCE to rise above.

Everyone will see Jesus
by the PATIENCE you so freely provide.
Letting others know your love for Jesus,
a love you will not hide.

Jesus tells us to show PATIENCE
to everyone we know.
So, listen to His words and
closer to Jesus you will grow.

PRAYER

Before we go, can we pray together and ask
for God's help in having PATIENCE?

Lord God,

Thank you that you freely give us PATIENCE as we believe in your Son, Jesus. Thank you for giving me your Spirit to help me have PATIENCE because I need your help every day to be patient with others. Help me remember how much PATIENCE you have with me. Show me new ways to have PATIENCE with others this week. Holy Spirit give me the power to act on what the Lord shows me. In Jesus' name, I pray all these things. Amen.

Discussion questions for parents and grandparents with their children and grandchildren:

🍑 What is the first thing that comes to mind when you ask God to show you a way to have PATIENCE with others?

🍑 Will you commit to doing it?

Here's a fun idea: You can use a light orange beaded bracelet to remind you of God's PATIENCE for you and to share His PATIENCE with others. If you don't have one, you can make your own bracelet with light orange beads.

Enjoy watching a video of this devotion online by using this link:
https://vimeo.com/201848884

Or by scanning the QR code below:

Fruit of the Spirit:
KINDNESS

Hello there, boys and girls!
My name is Simon Ekai.

I live in Nyahururu, Kenya in Africa at The
Home of the Good Shepherd. Today I would
like to share with you what I have learned
about KINDNESS by living with many other
children.

PRAYER

Let's open with a short prayer:

Lord God, please give us ears to hear you speaking to us through this devotional and a heart that is willing to learn. Amen.

DEVOTIONAL

At The Home of the Good Shepherd, I can find ways to show KINDNESS to someone many times a day. I do have to admit that even though the Bible teaches us to show KINDNESS it isn't always easy for me. KINDNESS means I need to forgive my brothers and sisters when they have done something to hurt me. Thankfully God helps me forgive them.

KINDNESS also means I am willing to help my brothers and sisters with something even if I am busy playing outside or busy with something else. To show KINDNESS, I need the help of God the Father, Son and Holy Spirit or I could not succeed.

Let's look at God's word and see what it says about KINDNESS. Let's try to memorize this verse in Ephesians 4.

MEMORY VERSE

"Be kind and compassionate to one another, forgiving each other, just as in Christ God forgave you." (Ephesians 4:32)

POEM

Another fun way to learn about KINDNESS is to read through this poem. Poems help us remember.

If there is someone who has not been nice
or even mean to you,
Show them KINDNESS and let the love of
Jesus
shine brightly through.

Offering forgiveness is showing KINDNESS
when a friend has made you sad.
Letting them know you love and forgive them
will surely make them glad.

KINDNESS can be hard to share
but through the Holy Spirit's power,
You can rise above and let KINDNESS flow
like a gentle rain shower.

Jesus taught us KINDNESS as a way for us
to show others how much we care.
So, let KINDNESS fill you to overflowing
and the love of Jesus will fill the air.

PRAYER

Before we go, can we pray together and ask
for God's help in choosing to share our
KINDNESS?

Lord God,

Thank you that you freely give us KINDNESS as
we believe in your Son, Jesus. Thank you for
giving me your Spirit to help me have
KINDNESS. I need your help every day to share
KINDNESS with others and never be too busy
to help someone. Show me new ways to
share Your KINDNESS in me with others this
week. Holy Spirit give me the power to act on

what the Lord shows me. In Jesus' name, I pray all these things. Amen.

Discussion questions for parent and grandparents with their children and grandchildren:

What is the first thing that comes to mind when you ask God to show you a way to show KINDNESS to others?

Will you commit to doing it?

Here's a fun idea: You can use a bright pink beaded bracelet to remind you of God's KINDNESS to you and to show His KINDNESS to others. If you don't have one, you can make your own bracelet with bright pink beads.

Enjoy watching a video of this devotion online
by using this link:
https://vimeo.com/201854421

Or by scanning the QR code below

Fruit of the Spirit:
GOODNESS

Hello there, boys and girls!
My name is Grace Wanjiku.

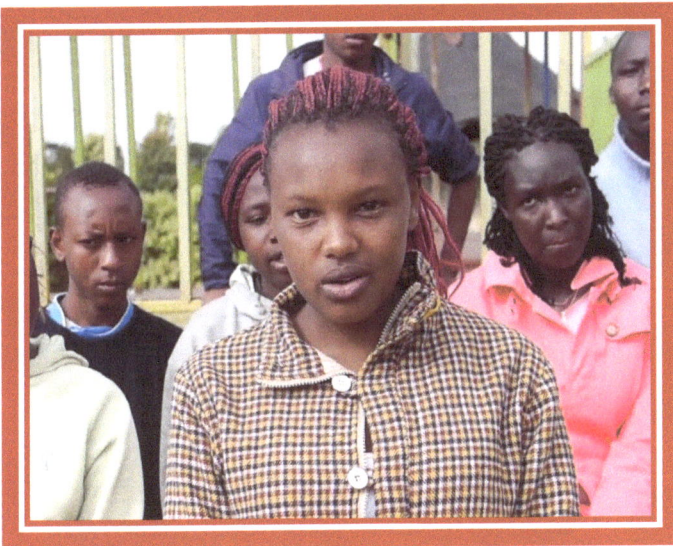

I live in Nyahururu, Kenya in Africa at The
Home of the Good Shepherd. Today I would
like to share with you what I have learned
about GOODNESS by living with many other
children.

PRAYER

Let's open with a short prayer:

Lord God, please give us ears to hear you speaking to us through this devotional and a heart that is willing to learn. Amen.

DEVOTIONAL

I am excited to talk to you today about GOODNESS because it is my favorite fruit of the Spirit! Some people get confused and think GOODNESS and KINDNESS are the same but they are definitely different. GOODNESS is not about *being* good, it is about *doing* good and pushing others to *do* good.

One way all of us at The Home of the Good Shepherd share GOODNESS is by taking food from our garden to other orphanages. You see, we have a huge garden and grow lots of tomatoes, cabbage, peppers and other vegetables. We know taking vegetables from our garden to these orphanages can help them have enough food to feed everyone who lives there. I am sure there are ways you share GOODNESS. Can you think of a way you can help someone in your school or neighborhood? Always remember God the Father, Son and Holy Spirit is there to help and support you!

Let's look at God's word and see what it says about GOODNESS. Let's try to memorize this verse in Galatians 6.

MEMORY VERSE

"Let us not become weary in doing good, for at the proper time we will reap a harvest if we do not give up." (Galatians 6:9)

POEM

Another fun way to learn about GOODNESS is to read through this poem. Poems help us remember.

GOODNESS is doing for others
what they cannot do for themselves,
Sharing what you have with others,
like toys or food from your shelves.
Wanting to hold on to everything
is selfish and not what we are to do.
Give freely of what you have to others
and the blessings will also be to you.

Jesus is there to guide you
when you see someone who is in need.
The Holy Spirit will help you show GOODNESS
and remove any greed.

GOODNESS is a gift we are to share
and to give away,
Letting others know Jesus loves them
every single day.

PRAYER

Before we go, can we pray together and ask
for God's help in choosing to share our
GOODNESS?

Lord God,

Thank you that you freely give us GOODNESS as we believe in your Son, Jesus. Thank you for giving me your Spirit to help me share GOODNESS. I need your help every day to share GOODNESS with others because there are so many people who need help. Show me new ways to share your GOODNESS in me with others this week. Holy Spirit give me the power to act on what the Lord shows me. In Jesus' name, I pray all these things. Amen.

Discussion questions for parents and grandparents with their children and grandchildren:

🍒 What is the first thing that comes to mind when you ask God to show you a way to show GOODNESS to others?

🍒 Will you commit to doing it?

Here's a fun idea: You can use a deep red beaded bracelet to remind you of God's GOODNESS to you and to show His GOODNESS to others. If you don't have one, you can make your own bracelet with deep red beads.

Enjoy watching a video of this devotion online by using this link:
https://vimeo.com/202167014

Or by scanning the QR code below

Fruit of the Spirit:
FAITHFULNESS

Hello there, boys and girls!
My name is Gladys Alkadel.

I live in Nyahururu, Kenya in Africa at The
Home of the Good Shepherd. Today I would
like to share with you what I have learned
about FAITHFULNESS by living with many other
children.

PRAYER

Let's open with a short prayer:

Lord God, please give us ears to hear you speaking to us through this devotional and a heart that is willing to learn. Amen.

DEVOTIONAL

Here at The Home of the Good Shepherd we all try to remain faithful to God and to each other. FAITHFULNESS to God can be described as loyalty to Him above everything else in your life. Sometimes I am tempted to be unfaithful by not reading my Bible or not telling others about Him. But then I remember God's FAITHFULNESS to me in sending His Son, Jesus, to die on the cross for my sins and it helps me to be more faithful to Him. I also remember times He has helped me out of some tough situations.

FAITHFULNESS to God can also be seen in FAITHFULNESS to others. Do your friends think of you as someone they can depend on? How about your parents? Are you obedient with what they ask you to do? God is dependable and He deserves all our trust and faith and He wants us to be worthy of trust as well.

Let's look at God's word and see what it has says about FAITHFULNESS. Let's try to memorize this verse in 1 Samuel 22.

MEMORY VERSE

"The Lord rewards everyone for their righteousness and faithfulness."
(1 Samuel 22:23)

POEM

Another fun way to learn about FAITHFULNESS is to read through this poem. Poems help us remember.

Jesus gave us the Ten Commandments
to help us live a life full of love.

When we break those rules, we are not being
faithful to our Father God above.
FAITHFULNESS means we can be trusted
to keep promises, staying true.
Being honest and truthful with others
and to always follow through.

The Holy Spirit will lead you
when you are tempted to stray from doing
your best.
Keeping your FAITHFULNESS to God
will show you have passed the test.

Your best is what Jesus asks for
in everything you do and say.
So, show FAITHFULNESS to everyone
where you live, learn and play.

PRAYER

Before we go, can we pray together and ask
for God's help in choosing FAITHFULNESS?

Lord God,

Thank you for being faithful to us by sending your Son, Jesus. Thank you for giving me your Spirit to help me be faithful. I need your help every day to be faithful to others and to you. Help me show my loyalty to you by reading my Bible, singing songs about you and talking about you to others. Help me also to be a faithful friend and child. Holy Spirit give me the power to act on what the Lord shows me. In Jesus' name, I pray all these things. Amen.

Discussion questions for parents and grandparents with their children and grandchildren:

What is the first thing that comes to mind when you ask God to show you a way to be faithful to Him and others?

Will you commit to doing it?

Here's a fun idea: You can use a green beaded bracelet to remind you of God's FAITHFULLNESS to you and to show His FAITHFULNESS to others. If you don't have one, you can make your own bracelet with green beads.

Enjoy watching a video of this devotion online by using this link:
https://vimeo.com/201666963

Or by scanning the QR code below

Fruit of the Spirit:
GENTLENESS

Hello there, boys and girls!
My name is Triza Wambuil.

I live in Nyahururu, Kenya in Africa at The
Home of the Good Shepherd. Today I would
like to share with you what I have learned
about GENTLENESS by living with many other
children.

PRAYER

Let's open with a short prayer:

Lord God, please give us ears to hear you speaking to us through this devotional and a heart that is willing to learn. Amen.

DEVOTIONAL

There are a lot of young children here at The Home of the Good Shepherd. It seems easier to be gentle with them than it is to be gentle with the older kids here. But the Bible says we are to be gentle to everyone. I am more likely to be gentle towards others if I don't think I am better than they are and don't have a know-it-all attitude.

I need the Holy Spirit to remind me to be gentle sometimes, especially if the boys and girls are being very loud and there is a lot going on around me. I think of how gentle Jesus must have been for the children to have wanted to gather around him when he said, "Let the little children come to me." in Matthew

19:14. I really want to be gentle to everyone because I know it is important to God.

Let's look at God's word and see what it says about GENTLENESS. Let's try to memorize this verse in Philippians 4.

MEMORY VERSE

"Let your gentleness be known to all men."
(Philippians 4:5)

POEM

Another fun way to learn about GENTLENESS is to read through this poem. Poems help us remember.

Be gentle in all things you say
and in all things you do,
To your friends and family
and to all the animals too.

When there is a lot of commotion
and you need GENTLENESS in your day,
Set yourself apart from the noise
and to the Holy Spirit pray.

Pray to Jesus that He gives you
the GENTLENESS you want to share.
Allowing you to show others
how much you really care

GENTLENESS in your words and actions
shows others Jesus is your guide.
Letting the light of Jesus shine brightly
through you
a light you will not hide.

PRAYER

Before we go, can we pray together and ask
for God's help to be gentle with everyone?

Lord God,

Thank you for giving us a good example of
GENTLENESS in Jesus. Thank you for giving me
your Spirit to help me be gentle to everyone. I
need your help every day to be gentle,

especially when others aren't. Help me not to think more of myself than I do of others or think my opinion counts more than anyone else's opinion. Please remind me to remain calm when things seem crazy so I can be gentle even then. In Jesus' name, I pray all these things. Amen.

Discussion questions for parents and grandparents with their children and grandchildren:

●● What is the first thing that comes to mind when you ask God to show you how to show GENTLENESS to others?

●● Will you commit to doing it?

Here's a fun idea: You can use an orange beaded bracelet to remind you of God's GENTLENESS to you and to show His GENTLENESS to others. If you don't have one, you can make your own bracelet with orange beads.

Enjoy watching a video of this devotion online
by using this link:

https://vimeo.com/202059038

Or by scanning the QR code below:

Fruit of the Spirit:
SELF-CONTROL

Hello there, boys and girls!
My name is Winnie Makena.

I live in Nyahururu, Kenya in Africa at The Home of the Good Shepherd. Today I would like to share with you what I have learned about SELF-CONROL by living with many other children.

Let's open with a short prayer:

Lord God, please give us ears to hear you speaking to us through this devotional and a heart that is willing to learn. Amen.

DEVOTIONAL

I think that SELF-CONTROL may be the easiest fruit of the Spirit to understand, but the hardest to do. To control something means to keep it within a certain boundary. If we are controlling a ball, we may struggle to keep it in certain boundary lines. When we are trying to control ourselves, it can also be a struggle.

One time people were visiting us from America and they gave us some candy. I really wanted to take more than my share of candy. We don't get the kind of candy they brought us very often here in Kenya, so I really had to use my SELF-CONTROL. It wasn't easy but I asked God for help and His Holy Spirit gave me the power to do the right thing.

Wow, it would have taken a lot of SELF-CONTROL for Jesus to do what His Father wanted Him to do when it was time to die on the cross. The issues I face seem very easy compared to that.

Let's look at God's word and see what it says about SELF-CONTROL. Let's try to memorize this verse in Titus 2.

MEMORY VERSE

"It (the Bible) teaches us to live self-controlled, upright, and godly lives in this present age." (Titus 2:12b)

POEM

Another fun way to learn about SELF-CONTROL is to read through this poem. Poems help us remember.

To have SELF-CONTROL is not something
we can do on our own.
We need Jesus and the Holy Spirit to lead us
at school and play and home.

When we live with SELF-CONTROL
we show how Jesus leads us throughout
our day.
And when we act out of control
it is clear we have lost our way.

Jesus is always there to bring us back
to a place of SELF-CONTROL.
All we need to do is pray for Jesus
to calm and restore our peaceful soul.

SELF-CONTROL requires discipline,
prayer and constant thought.
To remind us of how we are to live
by the lessons Jesus taught.

PRAYER

Before we go, can we pray together and ask
for God's help in using our SELF-CONTROL?

Lord God,

Thank you, Jesus, that you had so much SELF-CONTROL that you willingly died on the cross for us. Please help me to use my SELF-CONTROL in the situations I face. Thank you for giving me your Spirit to help me have SELF-CONTROL. I need your help every day to deny myself things that aren't good for me or for those around me, and to keep within the boundaries you have set for me. Holy Spirit give me the power to use my SELF-CONTROL. In Jesus' name, I pray all these things. Amen.

Discussion questions for parents and grandparents with their children and grandchildren:

🍋 What is the first thing that comes to mind when you ask God to show you a way to use your SELF-CONTROL when you are with others?

🍋 Will you commit to doing it?

Here's a fun idea: You can use a yellow beaded bracelet to remind you God will help you have SELF-CONTROL. If you don't have one, you can make your own bracelet with yellow beads.

Enjoy watching a video of this devotion online by using this link:
https://vimeo.com/202875305

Or by scanning the QR code below:

Hello!

We are excited to share a project with you that our Fruit That Lasts Ministry has been working on in conjunction with the Home of the Good Shepherd (HOTGS), an orphanage in Nyahururu, Kenya. The children and teenagers from the HOTGS have lovingly made children's bracelets that we have combined with a written devotion.

The devotions are based on the fruit of the Spirit – love, joy, peace, patience, kindness, goodness, faithfulness, gentleness and self-control. Each devotion and fruit of the Spirit has its own special color bracelet. When a reader completes a devotion, they are encouraged to wear the bracelet that corresponds with the devotion to help them remember to show that particular fruit of the Spirit throughout their day.

Once they have completed all nine devotions, the reward is that they are then able to wear all nine bracelets. Optionally, they may choose to wear the color bracelet that coincides with any fruit of the Spirit they are struggling with the most.

One of the most exciting aspects of the project is that for each fruit of the Spirit devotion there is a corresponding video that features the children from HOTGS. On the back of each written devotion we have a link to these videos and a QR Scan Code. To access the code, you simply hold your phone (with a free QR reader app previously installed) over the scan code and the HOTGS videos will pop up on your phone. When you press play, a specially prepared video about that particular fruit of the Spirit begins---ALL THE WAY FROM KENYA!

We are so proud of the children at the HOTGS for all the hard work they have put into the bracelets and videos. They memorized each devotion, prayer, memory verse and poem for each fruit of the Spirit!

ALL profits will go to help with the education and living expenses of the HOTGS children. Praise the Lord for this opportunity to help these precious children!

Blessings,

Kristi & Nena

Kristi Smith & Nena Jackson
Fruit That Lasts Ministry

www.ingramcontent.com/pod-product-compliance
Lightning Source LLC
Chambersburg PA
CBHW042107110426
42742CB00033BA/20